A companion to the Yom Kippur *machzor*

עַל חֵטְא שֶׁחָטָאנוּ לְפָנֶיךָ...

בְּאֹנֶס וּבְרָצוֹן : וְעַל חֵטְא שֶׁחָטָאנוּ לְפָנֶיךָ בְּאִמּוּץ הַלֵּב :
עַל חֵטְא שֶׁחָטָאנוּ לְפָנֶיךָ בִּבְלִי דָעַת : וְעַל חֵטְא שֶׁחָטָאנוּ לְפָנֶיךָ בְּבִטּוּי שְׂפָתָיִם :
עַל חֵטְא שֶׁחָטָאנוּ לְפָנֶיךָ בְּגָלוּי וּבַסֵּתֶר : וְעַל חֵטְא שֶׁחָטָאנוּ לְפָנֶיךָ בְּגִלּוּי עֲרָיוֹת :
עַל חֵטְא שֶׁחָטָאנוּ לְפָנֶיךָ בְּדַעַת וּבְמִרְמָה :
עַל חֵטְא שֶׁחָטָאנוּ לְפָנֶיךָ בְּהַרְהוֹר הַלֵּב : וְעַל חֵטְא שֶׁחָטָאנוּ לְפָנֶיךָ בְּהוֹנָאַת רֵעַ :
עַל חֵטְא שֶׁחָטָאנוּ לְפָנֶיךָ בְּוִעִידַת זְנוּת :
עַל חֵטְא שֶׁחָטָאנוּ לְפָנֶיךָ בְּזָדוֹן וּבִשְׁגָגָה : וְעַל חֵטְא שֶׁחָטָאנוּ לְפָנֶיךָ בְּזִלְזוּל הוֹרִים וּמוֹרִים :
עַל חֵטְא שֶׁחָטָאנוּ לְפָנֶיךָ בְּחֹזֶק יָד : וְעַל חֵטְא שֶׁחָטָאנוּ לְפָנֶיךָ בְּחִלּוּל הַשֵּׁם :
עַל חֵטְא שֶׁחָטָאנוּ לְפָנֶיךָ בְּטֻמְאַת שְׂפָתָיִם : וְעַל חֵטְא שֶׁחָטָאנוּ לְפָנֶיךָ בְּטִפְּשׁוּת פֶּה :
עַל חֵטְא שֶׁחָטָאנוּ לְפָנֶיךָ בְּיֵצֶר הָרָע : וְעַל חֵטְא שֶׁחָטָאנוּ לְפָנֶיךָ בְּיוֹדְעִים :
וְעַל כֻּלָּם אֱלוֹהַּ סְלִיחוֹת : סְלַח לָנוּ : מְחַל לָנוּ : כַּפֶּר לָנוּ בְּלַחַשׁ שְׁחַד :
וְעַל חֵטְא שֶׁחָטָאנוּ לְפָנֶיךָ בְּכַחַשׁ וּבְכָזָב : עַל חֵטְא שֶׁחָטָאנוּ לְפָנֶיךָ בְּלָשׁוֹן הָרָע :
וְעַל חֵטְא שֶׁחָטָאנוּ לְפָנֶיךָ בְּלָצוֹן : עַל חֵטְא שֶׁחָטָאנוּ לְפָנֶיךָ בְּמַשָּׂא וּבְמַתָּן :
עַל חֵטְא שֶׁחָטָאנוּ לְפָנֶיךָ בְּמַאֲכָל וּבְמִשְׁתֶּה : וְעַל חֵטְא שֶׁחָטָאנוּ לְפָנֶיךָ בְּנֶשֶׁךְ וּבְמַרְבִּית :
וְעַל חֵטְא שֶׁחָטָאנוּ לְפָנֶיךָ בִּנְטִיַּת גָּרוֹן : עַל חֵטְא שֶׁחָטָאנוּ לְפָנֶיךָ בְּשִׂקּוּר עָיִן :
וְעַל חֵטְא שֶׁחָטָאנוּ לְפָנֶיךָ בְּשִׂיחַ שִׂפְתוֹתֵינוּ : עַל חֵטְא שֶׁחָטָאנוּ לְפָנֶיךָ בְּעֵינַיִם רָמוֹת :
וְעַל חֵטְא שֶׁחָטָאנוּ לְפָנֶיךָ בְּעַזּוּת מֵצַח : וְעַל כֻּלָּם אֱלוֹהַּ סְלִיחוֹת.

...סְלַח לָנוּ. מְחַל לָנוּ. כַּפֶּר לָנוּ.

Adina Broder

Distributed by:
FELDHEIM PUBLISHERS
208 Airport Executive Park
Nanuet, NY 10954

Dedicated in loving memory of my parents,

Rabbi Saul & Rebbetzin Peggy Weiss

who encouraged me to publish an earlier version of this booklet when I first wrote it for my own children. I wish my parents were here to see this booklet in its improved and expanded form, as well as the impact it will hopefully have on all those who use it.

This booklet encompasses many of the principles that guided my parents' lives: spreading Hashem's message, inspiring children towards Judaism, and appreciating the incredible opportunity we have to speak to Hashem through our *tefilos*.

My parents were wonderful role models.
They didn't just learn Torah — they lived Torah.

Acknowledgements

I want to express my gratitude to my family for their continuous support and encouragement. In addition, their attention to detail in editing this booklet and their insightful comments and suggestions were invaluable.

Sources

The explanations in this booklet are based on translations and information from the Artscroll *machzor*, the "Viduy" pamphlet, Rambam's *Hilchos Shegagos* and *Hilchos Sanhedrin*, aish.com and Chabad.org.

בס"ד

קהילת נופי השמש, בית שמש ת"ו

רב שלום רוזנר

---

12 Menachem Av 5781

I have been shown a draft of "Viduy Booklet for Kids", organized and presented by Mrs. Adina Broder. Viduy is not only a challenging mitzva for us all, it is the centerpiece and anchor for the entire Yom Kippur davening. Mrs. Broder has done a tremendous service for our youth, by opening up to them much of the rabbinic concepts expressed in our vidui. She tries to capture the idea behind each line, with a focus on having practical teshuva messages for our children and grandchildren. May this booklet instill deep feelings of repentance in both young and old, and may we all merit to return to Hashem with all our heart.

With Torah Blessings,

Rabbi Shalom Rosner

Purpose of Viduy

In order for Hashem to forgive us for the things we did wrong, we need to go through a process called *teshuvah*. Part of this process is saying what our bad deeds were. To help us do this, the great rabbis prepared a *tefilah* which lists the most common sins. This *tefilah* is called *Viduy* (וִדּוּי). But simply uttering the words of *Viduy* isn't enough; one has to understand what he or she is saying. This booklet helps the reader by providing easy-to-understand explanations of the *Viduy tefilah*, along with kid-friendly examples.

Structure of Viduy

There are two parts to the *Viduy tefilah*: *Ashamnu*, which is a short list of *aveiros*, and *Al Cheit*, a more detailed version. Both lists follow the order of the *aleph-beis*. One reason for this is that when we sin, we go against the Torah which was written with the 22 letters of the *aleph-beis*. Therefore, we use all of those letters when asking for forgiveness.

How to Use this Booklet

This booklet works best when used while saying the *Viduy tefilah* during *davening*. Since this booklet contains all of the words from the beginning of *Viduy* until the end of *Shemonah Esrei*, the reader can set his or her *machzor* down when reaching the *Viduy tefilah* and use this booklet for the rest of *Shemonah Esrei*.[1]

---

[1] Those davening *nusach Sefard* will need to use their *machzor* for אֱלֹקַי נְצוֹר.

Note to Parents

This booklet generally does not contain exact translations for the *tefilos* that are included herein. Instead, it imparts the significance of the words in the clearest and most concise way possible in order to make the *davening* most accessible and meaningful to children.

There are some topics in the *Viduy tefilah* that have mature themes. Care was taken to address these topics with sensitivity and to adapt them in a way that focuses on the aspects that would be relevant to children.

Note to Kids

You should not rush through the *Viduy tefilah* or say the words without thinking about their meaning. Instead, take your time and reflect on how the *aveiros* that are listed might apply to you.

The *Viduy tefilah* lists the sins that people often commit. If there are things you did wrong that aren't mentioned in *Viduy*, you are allowed, and even encouraged, to add them into your *davening*.

Another thing to remember is that saying *Viduy* is just one step in having Hashem forgive your bad deeds. If you did wrong to another person, you need to ask that person for forgiveness before Hashem will forgive the sin. Apologizing can be difficult and sometimes awkward. Still, if you mistreated someone, Hashem requires that you say you're sorry to that person. This shows Him that you truly feel bad about what you did.

Lastly, saying what you did wrong is important. Even more important is working on changing bad behaviors in order to become the best person you can possibly be.

Beginning of the *Viduy Tefilah*

> The proper way to say *Viduy* is while standing and bending forward slightly.

אֱלֹהֵינוּ וֵאלֹהֵי אֲבוֹתֵינוּ, תָּבֹא לְפָנֶיךָ תְּפִלָּתֵנוּ, וְאַל תִּתְעַלַּם מִתְּחִנָּתֵנוּ,

שֶׁאֵין אֲנַחְנוּ עַזֵּי פָנִים וּקְשֵׁי עֹרֶף לוֹמַר לְפָנֶיךָ יהוה אֱלֹהֵינוּ וֵאלֹהֵי

אֲבוֹתֵינוּ צַדִּיקִים אֲנַחְנוּ וְלֹא חָטָאנוּ אֲבָל אֲנַחְנוּ וַאֲבוֹתֵינוּ חָטָאנוּ.

Hashem, please listen to my *tefilos*. I am not pretending that I have been
perfect or that I haven't sinned. Instead, I am admitting that I have done things
wrong and want Your forgiveness.

Ashamnu

> As each phrase is said, lightly hit the left side of the chest with one's fist.

BEING GUILTY - אָשַׁמְנוּ

I admit that I did things that were wrong.

BEING DISLOYAL - בָּגַדְנוּ

By doing *aveiros*, I was disloyal to Hashem
and was ungrateful for all the good He does for me.

STEALING - גָּזַלְנוּ

I have taken things that don't belong to me. This includes using someone's
property without permission, purposely disturbing someone's sleep,
and eating without making a *brachah*.

דִּבַּרְנוּ דֹּפִי – SPEAKING IMPROPERLY

I have spoken *lashon hara*, talked about people behind their backs, and complained about Hashem and the *mitzvos*.

הֶעֱוִינוּ – CAUSING OTHERS TO DO BAD

I have spoken or acted in a way that has led others to act improperly.

וְהִרְשַׁעְנוּ – CAUSING OTHERS TO BE WICKED

I caused others to hurt people or to plan how to do something wrong.

זַדְנוּ – SINNING ON PURPOSE

I did bad things on purpose, despite knowing that it was wrong. Even worse, I made up reasons and excuses to justify sinning.

חָמַסְנוּ – TAKING ADVANTAGE OF PEOPLE

I forced or pressured others to give me things that I knew they didn't really want to give me.

טָפַלְנוּ שֶׁקֶר – ACCUSING OTHERS FALSELY

I lied about other people or accused them falsely.

יָעַצְנוּ רָע – GIVING BAD ADVICE

I knowingly gave people advice that wasn't good for them — sometimes for my own benefit.

LYING - כִּזַּבְנוּ

I cheated, lied, or made people think things that weren't true.
I made promises that I didn't plan to keep.

MOCKING - לַצְנוּ

I joked about things that should be taken seriously.
I also made fun of people or the Torah.

REBELLING - מָרַדְנוּ

I went against Hashem's Torah on purpose,
even when recognizing that He is the Creator and Master of the world.

ANGERING HASHEM - נִאַצְנוּ

I acted disrespectfully towards Hashem and the Torah.

TURNING AWAY FROM HASHEM - סָרַרְנוּ

I have ignored what Hashem wants me to do
and didn't keep some of His *mitzvos*.

ACTING IMPROPERLY - עָוִינוּ

I let myself speak or act improperly.
I hung out with people who I knew would be a bad influence on me.

DENYING THAT EVERY MITZVAH IS VALID - פָּשַׁעְנוּ

I didn't keep a *mitzvah* because I didn't think it was important.

HURTING OTHERS - צָרַרְנוּ

I caused physical or emotional pain to someone.
I didn't try to help someone who was hurt or sad.

BEING STUBBORN - קִשִּׁינוּ עֹרֶף

I refused to see Hashem in my life or in the world.
Also, I haven't tried to become a better person.

ACTING BADLY – רָשַׁעְנוּ

I have hit someone, stolen, or planned how to do something wrong.
And worse, I have been proud of my bad actions instead of ashamed of them.

DEVELOPING BAD TRAITS - שִׁחַתְנוּ

I acted as if I were better than other people. I let myself get very angry
instead of controlling my anger. I ignored the needs of others.

HURTING ONE'S CHARACTER - תִּעַבְנוּ

I acted badly often, not realizing how my actions affected
the type of person I was becoming.

STRAYING FROM HASHEM - תָּעִינוּ

I started drifting away from Hashem
and didn't make Him a part of my everyday life.

ALLOWING US TO STRAY- תִּעְתָּעְנוּ

I didn't turn to Hashem when I needed help.
I didn't care that I was ignoring my relationship with Hashem.

סַרְנוּ מִמִּצְוֹתֶיךָ וּמִמִּשְׁפָּטֶיךָ הַטּוֹבִים וְלֹא שָׁוָה לָנוּ. וְאַתָּה צַדִּיק עַל כָּל הַבָּא עָלֵינוּ כִּי אֱמֶת עָשִׂיתָ וַאֲנַחְנוּ הִרְשָׁעְנוּ.

I have turned away from Your *mitzvos*, Hashem. You are correct in everything that You do. I, on the other hand, have done wrong.

מַה נֹּאמַר לְפָנֶיךָ יוֹשֵׁב מָרוֹם, וּמַה נְּסַפֵּר לְפָנֶיךָ שׁוֹכֵן שְׁחָקִים, הֲלֹא כָּל הַנִּסְתָּרוֹת וְהַנִּגְלוֹת אַתָּה יוֹדֵעַ.

What can I say in defense of my bad deeds? I can't hide anything from You because You know the truth.

During *Ne'ilah*, in the last *Shemonah Esrei* of Yom Kippur, *Viduy* ends here. Continue in your *machzor* with "אַתָּה נוֹתֵן יַד".

אַתָּה יוֹדֵעַ רָזֵי עוֹלָם, וְתַעֲלוּמוֹת סִתְרֵי כָל חָי. אַתָּה חוֹפֵשׂ כָּל חַדְרֵי בָטֶן, וּבוֹחֵן כְּלָיוֹת וָלֵב. אֵין דָּבָר נֶעְלָם מִמֶּךָּ, וְאֵין נִסְתָּר מִנֶּגֶד עֵינֶיךָ. וּבְכֵן יְהִי רָצוֹן מִלְפָנֶיךָ, יהוה אֱלֹהֵינוּ וֵאלֹהֵי אֲבוֹתֵינוּ, שֶׁתִּסְלַח לָנוּ עַל כָּל חַטֹּאתֵינוּ, וְתִמְחָל לָנוּ עַל כָּל עֲוֹנוֹתֵינוּ, וּתְכַפֵּר לָנוּ עַל כָּל פְּשָׁעֵינוּ.

You, Hashem, know my actions, thoughts, and feelings, so I can't pretend that I didn't do wrong or that I had a good excuse. Please forgive all my sins.

Al Cheit

Some hit the left side of the chest with their fist each time the word "חֵטְא" is said. Others strike their chest when the word "שֶׁחָטָאנוּ" is said.

SINNING WHEN FEELING FORCED AND SINNING WILLINGLY

עַל חֵטְא שֶׁחָטָאנוּ לְפָנֶיךָ בְּ**אֹ**נֶס וּבְרָצוֹן,

I am sorry for the times that I did something wrong because I felt like I had to —
for example, because my friends were doing it. And I am sorry for the times
that I did something wrong just because I wanted to do it.

HAVING A HARD HEART

וְעַל חֵטְא שֶׁחָטָאנוּ לְפָנֶיךָ בְּ**אִ**מּוּץ הַלֵּב.

I am sorry for the times that I acted stubbornly and for refusing to admit
when I was wrong. I am also sorry for not helping people more
and not doing *chesed* more often.

SINNING DUE TO LACK OF KNOWLEDGE

עַל חֵטְא שֶׁחָטָאנוּ לְפָנֶיךָ בִּ**בְ**לִי דָעַת,

I am sorry for not studying Torah more and not paying attention when being
taught. This led me to sin, because I didn't know the correct *halachos*.

NOT THINKING BEFORE SPEAKING

וְעַל חֵטְא שֶׁחָטָאנוּ לְפָנֶיךָ בְּ**בִ**טּוּי שְׂפָתָיִם.

I am sorry for the times that I spoke without thinking which caused someone's
feelings to be hurt. I am also sorry for the times I whined or complained.

SINNING PUBLICLY & PRIVATELY

עַל חֵטְא שֶׁחָטָאנוּ לְפָנֶיךָ בְּגָלוּי וּבַסָּתֶר,

I am sorry for the times I didn't care that what I was doing was wrong,
and I did it in front of everyone. And I am sorry for the times
that I did something wrong when I thought no one was watching,
forgetting that Hashem sees everything.

ACTING INAPPROPRIATELY

וְעַל חֵטְא שֶׁחָטָאנוּ לְפָנֶיךָ בְּגִלוּי עֲרָיוֹת.

I am sorry for the times that I acted inappropriately
or read a book or magazine that wasn't appropriate.

SPEAKING HARSHLY

עַל חֵטְא שֶׁחָטָאנוּ לְפָנֶיךָ בְּדִבּוּר פֶּה,

I am sorry for the times that I said mean things to someone.
And I am sorry for the times that I spoke harshly or rudely to someone.

USING TRICKERY

וְעַל חֵטְא שֶׁחָטָאנוּ לְפָנֶיךָ בְּדַעַת וּבְמִרְמָה.

I am sorry for the times that I played a mean trick on someone.

PLANNING TO SIN

עַל חֵטְא שֶׁחָטָאנוּ לְפָנֶיךָ בְּהַרְהוֹר הַלֵּב,

I am sorry for the times that I planned how to do something wrong
or how to be mean to someone.

BETRAYING A FRIEND

וְעַל חֵטְא שֶׁחָטָאנוּ לְפָנֶיךָ בְּ**ה**וֹנָאַת רֵעַ.

I am sorry for the times that I took advantage of someone or broke their trust.

APOLOGIZING INSINCERELY

עַל חֵטְא שֶׁחָטָאנוּ לְפָנֶיךָ בְּ**ו**ִדּוּי פֶּה,

I am sorry for the times that I apologized but didn't really mean it.

BEHAVING IMMODESTLY

וְעַל חֵטְא שֶׁחָטָאנוּ לְפָנֶיךָ בְּ**ו**ַעִידַת זְנוּת.

I am sorry for the times that I acted in ways that didn't follow the laws of *tznius*.

SINNING ON PURPOSE & BY ACCIDENT

עַל חֵטְא שֶׁחָטָאנוּ לְפָנֶיךָ בְּ**ז**ָדוֹן וּבִשְׁגָגָה,

I am sorry for the times that I did something wrong on purpose and for the times that I did something wrong by mistake due to my carelessness.

BEING DISRESPECTFUL

וְעַל חֵטְא שֶׁחָטָאנוּ לְפָנֶיךָ בְּ**ז**ִלְזוּל הוֹרִים וּמוֹרִים.

I am sorry for the times that I wasn't respectful to my parents or teachers.

BULLYING

עַל חֵטְא שֶׁחָטָאנוּ לְפָנֶיךָ בְּ**ח**וֹזֶק יָד,

I am sorry for the times that I hit, kicked, or shoved someone.
I am sorry for the times that I bullied someone or didn't interfere when another person was being bullied.

MAKING A *CHILUL HASHEM*

וְעַל חֵטְא שֶׁחָטָאנוּ לְפָנֶיךָ בְּ**ח**לּוּל הַשֵּׁם.

I am sorry for the times that I did not behave properly in public, which could make people think poorly of Jewish people, the Torah, or Hashem.

SPEAKING FOOLISHLY

עַל חֵטְא שֶׁחָטָאנוּ לְפָנֶיךָ בְּ**ט**פְשׁוּת פֶּה,

I am sorry for the times that I was joking around in a way that hurt someone else's feelings.

SPEAKING INAPPROPRIATELY

וְעַל חֵטְא שֶׁחָטָאנוּ לְפָנֶיךָ בְּ**ט**מְאַת שְׂפָתַיִם.

I am sorry for the times that I said improper words, including telling an inappropriate joke or singing lyrics of a song that weren't appropriate.

LISTENING TO ONE'S *YETZER HARA*

עַל חֵטְא שֶׁחָטָאנוּ לְפָנֶיךָ בְּ**י**ֵצֶר הָרָע,

I am sorry for the times that I put myself in a situation where I knew I would end up doing something wrong.

SINNING AGAINST SOMEONE WHO MAY NOT BE AWARE OF IT

וְעַל חֵטְא שֶׁחָטָאנוּ לְפָנֶיךָ בְּ**י**וֹדְעִים וּבְלֹא יוֹדְעִים.

I am sorry for the times that I was mean to someone right to their face and for times that I was mean behind their back.

וְעַל כֻּלָּם אֱלוֹהַּ סְלִיחוֹת. סְלַח לָנוּ. מְחַל לָנוּ. כַּפֶּר לָנוּ.

For all of these things, I am very sorry, and I will try to do better. Hashem, please forgive me.

BRIBING

עַל חֵטְא שֶׁחָטָאנוּ לְפָנֶיךָ בְּ**כַ**פַּת שֹׁחַד,

I am sorry for the times that I pretended to be nice to someone
or complimented them just so they would give me something.

BEING DISHONEST

וְעַל חֵטְא שֶׁחָטָאנוּ לְפָנֶיךָ בְּ**כַ**חַשׁ וּבְכָזָב.

I am sorry for the times that I did not tell the truth
or deceived people by letting them think something that wasn't true.

SPEAKING *LASHON HARA*

עַל חֵטְא שֶׁחָטָאנוּ לְפָנֶיךָ בְּ**לָ**שׁוֹן הָרָע,

I am sorry for the times that I said bad things about someone
without a valid reason.

MOCKING

וְעַל חֵטְא שֶׁחָטָאנוּ לְפָנֶיךָ בְּ**לָ**צוֹן.

I am sorry for the times that I made fun of a person,
a *mitzvah*, or Judaism.

DEALING UNFAIRLY

עַל חֵטְא שֶׁחָטָאנוּ לְפָנֶיךָ בְּ**מַ**שָׂא וּבְמַתָּן,

I am sorry for the times that I made a deal that I knew was bad
for the other person. One example is when sharing something,
purposely not splitting it evenly.

SINNING WITH REGARD TO FOOD

וְעַל חֵטְא שֶׁחָטָאנוּ לְפָנֶיךָ בְּ**מַ**אֲכָל וּבְמִשְׁתֶּה.

I am sorry for the times that I ate food that I wasn't sure was kosher.
Also for not always waiting the proper amount of time between eating
milk and meat (according to my family's *minhag*). I am sorry for the times
that I didn't make a *brachah* before or after eating or drinking.
Also, sometimes I didn't wash before eating bread.

LENDING UNFAIRLY

עַל חֵטְא שֶׁחָטָאנוּ לְפָנֶיךָ בְּ**נֶ**שֶׁךְ וּבְמַרְבִּית,

I am sorry for the times that I lent something (money or a snack) and asked the
person to pay me back more than the amount that I had given.

BRAGGING

וְעַל חֵטְא שֶׁחָטָאנוּ לְפָנֶיךָ בִּ**נְ**טִיַּת גָּרוֹן.

I am sorry for the times that I bragged, showed off,
or acted as if I were better than others.

SINNING WITH ONE'S EYES

עַל חֵטְא שֶׁחָטָאנוּ לְפָנֶיךָ בְּ**שִׂ**קּוּר עָיִן,

I am sorry for the times that I looked at something private that someone else
had written. Some examples are looking at someone else's diary, homework, or
test, when I wasn't given permission or when it wasn't allowed.

NOT HAVING *KAVANAH*

וְעַל חֵטְא שֶׁחָטָאנוּ לְפָנֶיךָ בְּ**שִׂ**יחַ שִׂפְתוֹתֵינוּ.

I am sorry for the times that I *davened* or said *birkas hamazon* without
concentrating on what I was saying.

LOOKING DOWN ON PEOPLE

עַל חֵטְא שֶׁחָטָאנוּ לְפָנֶיךָ בְּ**עֵי**נַיִם רָמוֹת,

I am sorry for the times that I made someone feel bad about themselves —
perhaps because they didn't play sports well, do well on a test,
or wear nice clothing.

NOT FEELING EMBARRASSED TO SIN

וְעַל חֵטְא שֶׁחָטָאנוּ לְפָנֶיךָ בְּ**עַ**זּוּת מֵצַח.

I am sorry for the times I didn't feel ashamed when doing something wrong.

וְעַל כֻּלָּם אֱלוֹהַ סְלִיחוֹת. סְלַח לָנוּ. מְחַל לָנוּ. כַּפֶּר לָנוּ.

For all of these things, I am very sorry, and I will try to do better.
Hashem, please forgive me.

NOT ACTING RESPONSIBLY

עַל חֵטְא שֶׁחָטָאנוּ לְפָנֶיךָ בִּ**פְ**רִיקַת עֹל,

I am sorry for the times that I didn't do my fair share, which made someone
else have to work harder — such as when I didn't clean up my mess, so
someone else had to do it.

JUDGING OTHERS

וְעַל חֵטְא שֶׁחָטָאנוּ לְפָנֶיךָ בִּ**פְ**לִילוּת.

I am sorry for the times I judged someone without knowing the whole story.
I am also sorry for accusing someone of doing something wrong when I didn't
know for sure if they had done it.

TRICKING A FRIEND

עַל חֵטְא שֶׁחָטָאנוּ לְפָנֶיךָ בִּצְדִיַת רֵעַ,

I am sorry for the times that I convinced a friend to do something that I knew was wrong.

BEING JEALOUS

וְעַל חֵטְא שֶׁחָטָאנוּ לְפָנֶיךָ בְּצָרוּת עָיִן.

I am sorry for the times I felt bad about something good happening to someone else because I wished it had happened to me instead.

ACTING IMMATURELY

עַל חֵטְא שֶׁחָטָאנוּ לְפָנֶיךָ בְּקַלוּת ראשׁ,

I am sorry I joked around or acted silly when it wasn't the right time for it.

ACTING STUBBORNLY

וְעַל חֵטְא שֶׁחָטָאנוּ לְפָנֶיךָ בְּקַשִׁיוּת עֹרֶף.

I am sorry for the times that I refused to change my bad behavior, even when others showed me I was wrong.

RUSHING TO DO A SIN

עַל חֵטְא שֶׁחָטָאנוּ לְפָנֶיךָ בְּרִיצַת רַגְלַיִם לְהָרַע,

I am sorry for the times I was excited to do something wrong.

GOSSIPING

וְעַל חֵטְא שֶׁחָטָאנוּ לְפָנֶיךָ בִּרְכִילוּת.

I am sorry for the times I told embarrassing or private stories about someone.

PROMISING FALSELY

עַל חֵטְא שֶׁחָטָאנוּ לְפָנֶיךָ בִּ**שְׁ**בוּעַת שָׁוְא,

I am sorry for the times that I made a promise that I did not plan on keeping.

HATING ANOTHER

וְעַל חֵטְא שֶׁחָטָאנוּ לְפָנֶיךָ בְּ**שִׂ**נְאַת חִנָּם.

I am sorry for the times that I was mean to someone for no reason — such as excluding someone from a game or activity. Also, I am sorry for the times that I did something for the sole purpose of annoying my friend or sibling.

ACTING SELFISHLY

עַל חֵטְא שֶׁחָטָאנוּ לְפָנֶיךָ בִּ**תְ**שׂוּמֶת יָד,

I am sorry for not sharing more. I am also sorry for not giving the proper amount of my money to *tzedakah* (which is 10% of money I earn or receive).

NOT RECOGNIZING HASHEM

וְעַל חֵטְא שֶׁחָטָאנוּ לְפָנֶיךָ בְּ**תִ**מְהוֹן לֵבָב.

I am sorry for the times that I didn't see Hashem in my life
or forgot that Hashem has a reason for everything that happens.

וְעַל כֻּלָּם אֱלוֹהַ סְלִיחוֹת. סְלַח לָנוּ. מְחַל לָנוּ. כַּפֶּר לָנוּ.

For all of these things, I am very sorry, and I will try to do better.
Hashem, please forgive me.

The alphabetical list of sins is completed. Next, we list the *korbanos* and punishments that would have been given for some *aveiros*, were we to still have the *Beis Hamikdash*. Even though we are no longer obligated in these *korbanos* and punishments, we mention them in our *davening* in order to help us focus on what we did wrong and to remind us of the need to do *teshuvah*.

Some have the custom not to hit their chest while saying the following list. Others lightly hit the left side of their chest as they say the word "חֲטָאִים".

וְעַל חֲטָאִים שֶׁאָנוּ חַיָּבִים עֲלֵיהֶם עוֹלָה.

I am sorry for not keeping a positive *mitzvah*,
which is a law that tells us to do something.
This includes not: honoring one's parents, returning a lost object,
putting on *tefillin*, or saying *birkas hamazon*.

וְעַל חֲטָאִים שֶׁאָנוּ חַיָּבִים עֲלֵיהֶם חַטָּאת.

I am sorry for doing *aveiros* by mistake,
like accidentally violating Shabbos.

וְעַל חֲטָאִים שֶׁאָנוּ חַיָּבִים עֲלֵיהֶם עוֹלֶה וְיוֹרֵד.

I am sorry for making false promises and lying.

וְעַל חֲטָאִים שֶׁאָנוּ חַיָּבִים עֲלֵיהֶם אָשָׁם וַדַּאי וְתָלוּי.

I am sorry for taking something that belonged
to someone else without permission.

וְעַל חֲטָאִים שֶׁאָנוּ חַיָּבִים עֲלֵיהֶם מַכַּת מַרְדּוּת.

I am sorry for going against a *mitzvah d'rabannan*,
which is a law that the Rabbis commanded.
This includes not making a *brachah* before eating or drinking,
and not washing before having bread.

וְעַל חֲטָאִים שֶׁאָנוּ חַיָּבִים עֲלֵיהֶם מַלְקוּת אַרְבָּעִים.

I am sorry for going against a negative *mitzvah*,
which is a law that tells us not to do something.
This includes hitting someone, speaking *lashon hara*,
and eating non-kosher.

וְעַל חֲטָאִים שֶׁאָנוּ חַיָּבִים עֲלֵיהֶם מִיתָה בִּידֵי שָׁמָיִם.

I am sorry for making fun of the Torah or the Rabbis.

וְעַל חֲטָאִים שֶׁאָנוּ חַיָּבִים עֲלֵיהֶם כָּרֵת וַעֲרִירִי.

I am sorry for doing certain *aveiros* on purpose, like eating on
Yom Kippur (except when it's allowed) and eating *chameitz* on Pesach.

וְעַל חֲטָאִים שֶׁאָנוּ חַיָּבִים עֲלֵיהֶם אַרְבַּע מִיתוֹת בֵּית דִּין
סְקִילָה שְׂרֵפָה הֶרֶג וְחֶנֶק.

I am sorry for purposely violating Shabbos or
purposely injuring my parents.

עַל מִצְוַת עֲשֵׂה וְעַל מִצְוַת לֹא תַעֲשֵׂה. בֵּין שֶׁיֵּשׁ בָּהּ קוּם עֲשֵׂה. וּבֵין שֶׁאֵין בָּהּ קוּם עֲשֵׂה. אֶת הַגְּלוּיִים לָנוּ וְאֶת שֶׁאֵינָם גְּלוּיִים לָנוּ. אֶת הַגְּלוּיִים לָנוּ כְּבָר אֲמַרְנוּם לְפָנֶיךָ. וְהוֹדִינוּ לְךָ עֲלֵיהֶם. וְאֶת שֶׁאֵינָם גְּלוּיִים לָנוּ לְפָנֶיךָ הֵם גְּלוּיִים וִידוּעִים. כַּדָּבָר שֶׁנֶּאֱמַר הַנִּסְתָּרֹת לַיהוה אֱלֹהֵינוּ. וְהַנִּגְלֹת לָנוּ וּלְבָנֵינוּ עַד עוֹלָם. לַעֲשׂוֹת אֶת כָּל דִּבְרֵי הַתּוֹרָה הַזֹּאת. כִּי אַתָּה סָלְחָן לְיִשְׂרָאֵל וּמָחֳלָן לְשִׁבְטֵי יְשֻׁרוּן בְּכָל דּוֹר וָדוֹר וּמִבַּלְעָדֶיךָ אֵין לָנוּ מֶלֶךְ מוֹחֵל וְסוֹלֵחַ אֶלָּא אָתָּה.

Please forgive me for doing *aveiros* and for not doing some *mitzvos*. I am asking for forgiveness for the sins that I remember doing but also for those that I don't remember doing. Of course, Hashem, You know everything, so You know all of the things I did wrong. Please forgive me for all of them, since You are known as the G-d of forgiveness.

אֱלֹהַי, עַד שֶׁלֹּא נוֹצַרְתִּי אֵינִי כְדַאי, וְעַכְשָׁו שֶׁנּוֹצַרְתִּי כְּאִלוּ לֹא נוֹצַרְתִּי. עָפָר אֲנִי בְּחַיָּי. קַל וָחֹמֶר בְּמִיתָתִי. הֲרֵי אֲנִי לְפָנֶיךָ כִּכְלִי מָלֵא בוּשָׁה וּכְלִמָּה. יְהִי רָצוֹן מִלְּפָנֶיךָ יהוה אֱלֹהַי וֵאלֹהֵי אֲבוֹתַי שֶׁלֹּא אֶחֱטָא עוֹד. וּמַה שֶׁחָטָאתִי לְפָנֶיךָ מָרֵק בְּרַחֲמֶיךָ הָרַבִּים. אֲבָל לֹא עַל יְדֵי יִסּוּרִים וָחֳלָיִם רָעִים.

Hashem, please forgive me even though I am not worthy of being forgiven. I am embarrassed and ashamed of my bad behavior. Hashem, please help me avoid sinning in the future and forgive my past sins.

אֱ**לֹהַי,** נְצוֹר לְשׁוֹנִי מֵרָע וּשְׂפָתַי מִדַּבֵּר מִרְמָה וְלִמְקַלְלַי נַפְשִׁי
תִדּוֹם וְנַפְשִׁי כֶּעָפָר לַכֹּל תִּהְיֶה פְּתַח לִבִּי בְּתוֹרָתֶךָ וּבְמִצְוֹתֶיךָ
תִּרְדּוֹף נַפְשִׁי וְכָל הַחוֹשְׁבִים עָלַי רָעָה מְהֵרָה הָפֵר עֲצָתָם וְקַלְקֵל
מַחֲשַׁבְתָּם. עֲשֵׂה לְמַעַן שְׁמֶךָ, עֲשֵׂה לְמַעַן יְמִינֶךָ, עֲשֵׂה לְמַעַן
קְדֻשָּׁתֶךָ, עֲשֵׂה לְמַעַן תּוֹרָתֶךָ. לְמַעַן יֵחָלְצוּן יְדִידֶיךָ הוֹשִׁיעָה יְמִינְךָ
וַעֲנֵנִי. יִהְיוּ לְרָצוֹן אִמְרֵי פִי וְהֶגְיוֹן לִבִּי לְפָנֶיךָ יהוה צוּרִי וְגוֹאֲלִי.

Take 3 steps back. Bow left and say: עֹשֶׂה הַשָּׁלוֹם בִּמְרוֹמָיו; bow right and say:
וְעַל כָּל יִשְׂרָאֵל וְאִמְרוּ אָמֵן ;bow forward and say: הוּא יַעֲשֶׂה שָׁלוֹם עָלֵינוּ.

עֹשֶׂה הַ**שָּׁלוֹם** בִּמְרוֹמָיו הוּא יַעֲשֶׂה שָׁלוֹם עָלֵינוּ וְעַל כָּל יִשְׂרָאֵל
וְאִמְרוּ אָמֵן.

Hashem, please prevent me from speaking improperly. Open my heart towards the Torah and help me want to do *mitzvos*. If there is someone who is planning to hurt me, please don't let them. Even if I am not worthy of Your help, I ask that You do it for Your sake and for the Torah's sake. I hope that my words and thoughts are acceptable to You.

Please bring peace for us and for all of Bnei Yisrael.

יְהִי רָצוֹן מִלְּפָנֶיךָ יהוה אֱלֹהֵינוּ וֵאלֹהֵי אֲבוֹתֵינוּ שֶׁיִּבָּנֶה בֵּית הַמִּקְדָּשׁ בִּמְהֵרָה
בְיָמֵינוּ וְתֵן חֶלְקֵנוּ בְּתוֹרָתֶךָ. וְשָׁם נַעֲבָדְךָ בְּיִרְאָה כִּימֵי עוֹלָם וּכְשָׁנִים
קַדְמוֹנִיּוֹת. וְעָרְבָה לַיהוה מִנְחַת יְהוּדָה וִירוּשָׁלָיִם כִּימֵי עוֹלָם וּכְשָׁנִים
קַדְמוֹנִיּוֹת.

Please let the *Beis Hamikdash* be rebuilt soon, so we can serve You the way we used to.

**Also by
Adina Broder**

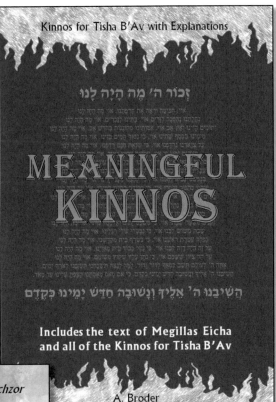

Kinnos for Tisha B'Av with Explanations

זְכוֹר ה' מֶה הָיָה לָנוּ

MEANINGFUL
KINNOS

הֲשִׁיבֵנוּ ה' אֵלֶיךָ וְנָשׁוּבָה חַדֵּשׁ יָמֵינוּ כְּקֶדֶם

Includes the text of Megillas Eicha
and all of the Kinnos for Tisha B'Av

A. Broder

A companion to the Yom Kippur *machzor*

עַל חֵטְא שֶׁחָטָאנוּ לְפָנֶיךָ ...

MEANINGFUL
VIDUY

...סְלַח לָנוּ. מְחַל לָנוּ. כַּפֶּר לָנוּ.

Adina Broder